AF510249

एहसास जो जिए गए

हार्दिक अनुभूति

Rooh Saidpuriya

BookLeaf Publishing

India | USA | UK

Made with ❤ on the BookLeaf Publishing Platform
www.bookleafpub.in
www.bookleafpub.com

Dedication

This book is dedicated to a little child who faced life bravely and was rewarded with courage, peace and satisfaction. To all the teenagers, young adults who choose to live life to it's fullest and keep their struggles to themselves, who believe in the beauty of LIFE, who know how to live with morality, who choose to be kind hearted and humble in their approach. To all those who finally choose happiness for themselves and come what may will always choose to be themselves.

Preface

The inspiration to write this book started with appreciation received by a class 6 student when the writer wrote her first piece and got praised by her Nana ji. Sadly, that poem is not in this collection as the poetess lost it. But as they say loosing something precious makes you value it more, the poetess ever since collected all her poems.

To be born in a house where emotions and feelings were very well appreciated, my bau ji reciting shayri out of boredom or sometimes to express his emotions for my b ji (grand mother), having parents who value lyrics in a song, created a culture of expression through words.

A few poems which overwhelmed me, felt so heavy that I choose to discard them while growing but very grateful to find a way of expression via writing. It's liberating, empowering and also a beautiful way to go through your journey.

There is a poem dedicated to my young cousin who works really hard to achieve her dream and that is my personal favorite.

Acknowledgements

I thank Bhagwan ji for instilling writing as medium of expression.

I thank my ancestors for blessing me as a courageous soul, my grandparents for being so loving that I value myself enough to express. A big thanks to my dear parents for believing in me.

Thanks to all the people I encountered on my way here, my dear brother, sister, cousins, uncle and aunt, my respected teachers for weaving my life with different colours, will forever be grateful to everybody for everything.

1. मन की अधूरी चाहत

मन में उठती हैं कुछ उमंगें
दब जाती है किसी की आहाट से
कुछ कहता है मन
नया करने को
कलम नहीं रुक्ति है
मन में प्रेरणा रहती है
जाने ये क्या कहती हैं
मन की आवाज़ें,
जी चाहता है कुछ नया कर दिखाऊँ
कितने हैं बेबस, जिन्हे
एक कागज़ तक नसीब नहीं होता |
जाने क्यों मन अचानक से
इन कल्पनाओं के गहरे सागर में डूब जाता है |
फिर अचानक लहर उठती है
नया जोश भर्ती है,
कलम की चाल तेज़ होती है
और अचानक रुक जाती है |

2. यादें

कब? किसी दिन,कहाँ की?
किस वक्त? कभी भी,
याद आती हैं।
कुछ स्मरण कराती हैं।
कभी घबराहट तो कभी
खुशियाँ लाती हैं।
किसी भी वक़्त
बिना बुलाएं आती हैं,
बस आती हैं और
चली जाती हैं।

3. माँ

इतना आम नहीं गहरे दुःख में मुस्कुराना
चार दीवारी से एक घर बनाना
सारे रिश्तें ज़िम्मेदारी से निभाना
बावजूद इन सबके अपनी शख्सियत कायम रख पाना
हस्ते हुए रसोई से कुछ मीठा खाना
दिन में ५ मिनट झपकी लेने का सच कभी न मानना
घर में सबसे छोटे होकर भी हक से सबकी डाट लगाना
खाना वही बनाना जो खुद हो खाना
उम्र के साथ अपनी ज़िद मनवाना
छोटी छोटी नई चीज़ो पर खुश होजाना
अपने खुशनुमा व्यक्तित्व से अपने आशियाने को गुलज़ार रख पाना
है अगर ये सब कहीं मुमकिन तो
परिचित हो इस आचरण की मूरत से
बेशक इन्हे माँ पुकार जाना |

4. FRIEND

Oh! to vent it to you
I waited for the weekend
then we talked and cried
over some past events.
Let's plan that outing
which we never execute
you too know it
I know it too.
Ya! finally
we are in a cafe
you spill the beans
till I sip my frappe.
Let the routine continue
till eternity.
Isn't just this wonderful,
I want nothing from you
and you too want it too.

5. राह

हौसला तूफानी है,
मंज़िल तो पानी है |
राह पर चल तो दिए
सिर्फ खुद का भरोसा साथ लिए |
ये जिद दूसरो की नहीं,
मेरे जूनून की कहानी है |
यकीनन सफर में मुश्किलें तमाम हैं,
परंतु जीत के जज़्बे में जो एहतराम है,
उसी स्वाद का दिल गुलाम है |

6. कुछ पल

फुर्सत के पल इतने तो खरीद ही लेना
की मशरूफियत में साँस ठहर के लो |
जब बारिश में कभी मन हो
तो बेशुमार काम काज के वजन में भी
परिवार के साथ चाय पी सको |
तबियत को इतना दुरुस्त रखना की
कोई नासाज़ हो तो उसके साथ खड़े हो सको,
और आखिर में इतना इल्म ज़रूर रखना
की आप ज़ात से इंसान ही हो |

7. भारत

एक मैं हूँ
बाकी सब जहाँ है |
और बचा सर पर मेरे मुल्क से परस्ती का नशा है
बस इतना ही पलसफ़ा है
मेरे अख़लाक़ से कही ज़्यादा मेरे लहू में भारत रमा है |

8. October to December

The warmth of room when you just wake up,
And chill when you get up,
It feels like it smells of early winters in morning.
The nostalgia hits,
Of beautiful sweaters and cardigans,
Of Aloo ka paratha and Chai.
The thought of reading favorite writers in quilt, give the indication
That dude! it's holidays season.
It's time when cousins return back to you,
It's time of greatest number of birthdays in a month.
It's time of lighting the house
And celebrating and reuniting with all those who left their nest to buy their own trees.
May we all succeed and
generations next to us,
Won't have to leave.
Happy winters!

9. मशरूफियत

आज काम का बोझ बोहोत ज्यादा था,
मेरा भी बस्ते को आसमान में फेंकने का इरादा था |
मैने मन से कहा गुनगुनाओ,
मुझे कोई बेहद खूबसूरत गीत सुनाओ,
में बैठी जो सुनने गीत,
मन बोला अभी तो बहुत काम है मीत |

10. संघर्ष

संघर्ष ही जीवन का सत्य है
आज संघर्ष है
कल यही हमे खुद्दार बनाएगा
जीवन में जो बुरा वक्त है,
वो कल नहीं आएगा |

11. सफलता

न जाने किस रंज से छूटे हैं आज
मुद्दत बाद ये ख़ुशी आयी है,
फुर्सत मिली है आज
तो होठों पर हसी छाई है |
दिल खुशनुमा हो याद करता है
आपकी दुआएँ भी हमने पाई हैं |
मुकम्मल हो गयी दुआ हमारी
शुरू हो गयी जशन की तैयारी|
मुसलसल चेहरे पर ये ख़ुमारी
हमारी मेहनत की हिस्सेदारी |

12. Moon

The breeze that gently pats my shoulder
In dreamy moonlight
Is an assurance by one high up there
That I have his back.
To the thoughts that were never written in my diary
Were shared with the moon
The best thing
They never required the reply
Oh! I can never in my dreams
Imagine something calmer than moon.
How come, something so far
Make me felt heard and
Things nearer never even bothered.
To that moon
My heart belongs.

13. कविता

कविता है मेरी आवाज़
जब में बोल नहीं पाती,
सुकून हैं लेख जब मै रोते हुए
कुछ कह नहीं पाती |
राहत है लिखाई
जब में हूँ घबराती,
कलम है रौशनी जब
मै अँधेरे में खो जाती |
कागज़ है तू
जब मै शिकवे सुनाती,
खुमारी है तू
जब मै बेवज़ह मुस्कुराती |
कामयाबी होगा मेरा ज़वाब
युही नहीं में बिन गलती सहे जाती,
कविता है मेरी जाती
जब मै नादान हो जिद्द पर आती |

14. दुआ

ऐ खुदा! अपनी नियामत मुझ पर भी बरसा |
अपने रहम-ओ-करम से हमें भी नवाज़,
हे परवरदिगार लेले अपनी पनाह में मुझे,
कुछ पल मुझे रूह का सुकून बक्श |
इस पल मौला करदे करम,
मेरे अपनों पर, मुझ पर|

15. सरल

न छल न कपट
गुब्बारे सा गुस्सा मेरा,
सोच समुद्र सी शांत ,
आत्मविश्वास जो आसमान छुए |
व्यवहार चमकता चाँद,
मन बिन माँझी की नाव सा,
फिर भी कोशिश लाख,
यकीन हिमालय सा अडिग |

16. Beautiful season

I am mostly the creation of my unconscious,
And when it surfaces through dream,
I slowly dwelve into the past,
The past that was lived beautifully, with best memories from college.
The place where I experienced freedom like never before,
Had my individual identity so strong,
In sea of countless new faces.
The joy that came from people knowing you
And yet they maintain distance.
Their's beauty in chivalry,
Who doesn't like this old world charm
Where people were not connected with social media,
Either they connected in reality
Or with admiration from afar.
This slow living,
Sitting in shade for hours with group of friends,
Attending all the departmental fests,
Being the group.
Standard of living was rich in sense

People used to know they all stay together
And had image that they will forever stay united in
every weather.
Little did I myself knew this was just a weather...

17. आशा

अपनी सोच हितकारी रख
अपना ख़्वाब अपने से ऊंचा रख
के अगर कभी तेरे पाव लड़खड़ायें
तो ये ही खूबसूरत ख़्वाब तेरी ताकत बन जायें |
है नहीं इस जग में कुछ तेरी सोच से विशाल
इसलिए अपनी सोच में रख उत्साह अपार
हो कभी तुझे तेरे नकरात्मक तू से सामना
अपने मन में सिर्फ एक लौ रख तू, सयम की संभाल |
किस अँधेरे में दम है जो रौशनी को टाल दे,
तेरा तेज यु हो की सौ और को संभाल दे |
चाहे पड़े तुझे, रोज़ खुद से जूझना
तो जूझ क्योंकि मुझे मंजूर नहीं,
तुझे यू टूटते देखना |
यकीन रख क्या हुआ
जो यूँ दो दिन घटा छा गई |
जान तू की सूरज है -
ले फिर धुप आ गई |

18. हमारे ही होगे

तुम जैसे भी होगे, जहा भी होगे,
हमारे ही होगे |
ख्वाहिश फलक की ही रखना
गिरे जमीं पर तब भी हमारे ही होगे |
न डरना अपनी उड़ान से, सितारों भरे आसमान से,
फैलाओ ये पंख निडर उड़ान के लिए
हारे जो मगर, जीते जो अगर
हर मौसम में बेफिक्र रहना
क्योंकि,
तुम जैसे भी होगे, जहा भी होगे,
हमारे ही होगे |

19. Journey from Volcano to Ice

I feel shackled
I feel chained
even working so hard
I am to be blamed
Life would have been easier
Had I been a bit selfish
This is the price
You pay for being caring
Blurting it out on paper
relaxes me as if my brain has got tranquilizer
but yes this is how I have made my life a little easier.
Cause otherwise I would have been just a complainer
but I'm proud of what I've become.
Your views won't define my reality
your opinion doesn't count my struggles
You are biased
Why should I be bothered
I feel good when I analyse your blame
they tell me that even in pain I

have raised my game.
I am a beautiful soul
not hurting others
rather calming your pain
calming my pain.

www.ingramcontent.com/pod-product-compliance
Lightning Source LLC
LaVergne TN
LVHW022033200926
848481LV00007B/2669